We Three The Trinity

by

Katherine Ranga

Illustration

by

Patrick Malalo-an

Inspiring Ministries

Copyright © 2020 Katherine Ranga

All rights reserved. No part of this publication may be reproduced, distributed, or transmitted in any form or by any means, including photocopying, recording, or other electronic or mechanical methods, without the prior written permission of the publisher, except in the case of brief quotations embodied in critical reviews and certain other noncommercial uses permitted by copyright law. For permission requests, write to the publisher, addressed "Attention: Permissions Coordinator," at the address below.

ISBN: 978-1-64871-919-6 (Electronic)
ISBN: 978-1-64871-935-6 (Paperback)

Front cover image by Patrick Malalo-an

First printing edition 2020.

Inspiring Ministries
Any enquiries are to be directed to Inspiring Ministries and the below e-mail address.
beinspired2read@gmail.com

www.inspiringministries.net.au

We Three The Trinity

Inspiring Ministries

We three they call, The Trinity...

God the Father, Jesus and Me.
They call me the Spirit,
Jesus the Son,
God the Father,
What we are is but ONE.

ONE heart,
ONE mind,
ONE soul, we have.

We made this world; We had a plan.
Our plan included you, you see,
You are to US the ultimate key.

You are Our LOVE; you're our precious ones.
We had a plan, that plan is not done

We want the best for you; you see...
God the Father, Jesus the Son and Me!

So don't forget us in your day,
at your friends or when you play.
We think of you and Our great plan,
for you to grow, be strong and stand...

For what is right and good in this world...
A little girl or a little boy.

Because you differ from adults, you see,
Your heart is pure, and that's the key.

To change a world that's hurt and old
into a world that's strong and bold.

WE will lead you when you speak,
as long as you continue to seek...

We Three, The Trinity.
God the Father, Jesus the Son and Me!

Made in the USA
Monee, IL
04 May 2026